Bleachfield

JA.S ROBERTSON ESQ.R

PROPERTY

College

Newmill

Grant Lodge

The Duke of Gordon

LD.S PROPERTY

Cathedral

Brewery

Major Duff

SEAFIELDS PROPERTY

Church

LORD SEAFIELDS PROPERTY

Road to Fochabers

Gray Friars

General Stewart King

Wynd

Maisondieu
Towns Property

Duncan's Close, early 20th century - Note thatched roof, in spite of ban in 1735

Elgin

The Story of the High Street and Closes

Mary Byatt

Published by The Moray Society

Published by
The Moray Society
The Elgin Museum,
1 High street, Elgin,
Moray. IV30 1EQ

© Mary Byatt, 2006

ISBN: 0-9554734-1-1 (2006)
ISBN: 978-0-9554734-1-8 (2007 onwards)

Printed by Highland Printers Limited
13 Henderson Road, Longmorn North,
Inverness IV1 1SP

For all who love Elgin
and especially David Byatt
who brought me to Moray

Acknowledgements

The author would like to express her sincere thanks to the Strathmartine Trust for major funding of this book and also The Moray Society and The Moray Council. Thanks are due to Richard Bennett, Elizabeth Beaton and Sarah Byatt for help with the text and to David Addison, Curator of the Elgin Museum, for help with design and layout. Graeme Wilson and Margaret Heron of the Moray Council Local Heritage Centre have been an invaluable source of information. Old photographs were supplied by both the Elgin Museum and the Heritage Centre.

Contents

Red Lion Close, 44 High Street

INTRODUCTION

The original aim of this book was to record what was left of Elgin's medieval closes in 2005/6 and so update the books written by Dr Ronald Cant, entitled *Old Elgin* (1946 and 1954) and *Historic Elgin and its Cathedral* (1974). At first I was not intending to include the High Street, but in studying the closes it became obvious that changes in the High Street itself were an integral part of the story and would have to be included. Details of the Cathedral, the Tolbooth, Old St Giles and the Plainstones have been omitted.

Elgin has a wealth of carved stones in the walls of its buildings, often re-used from previous buildings. Some came from the ruined cathedral. Others from the many High Street buildings that were replaced over the centuries. There are numerous decorated pediments, marriage stones, and heraldic carvings. Their history is often obscure. Robert Young, (*Annals of Elgin* 1879), described the old High Street buildings that had been destroyed in the 19th century. The Georgian and Victorian buildings that replaced them are themselves now of historic value and have a story all of their own. Many are uninhabited on the upper floors and in a poor state of repair, with vegetation growing unchecked at roof level. These buildings need recording too before they in turn are replaced. They deserve more space than I have been able to give them.

It is hard to imagine each close off the High Street teeming with large families, but so it was in the 19th century. The population remained concentrated in the centre until well into the 20th century. Nowadays only a few of the remaining closes are inhabited. In many closes the buildings are used for commercial purposes or for storage. Most closes are now cluttered with wheelie bins.

There is no record of when the High Street was originally numbered, but it is known that numbering started on one side in the west end, went all the way along one side and back up the other side. This resulted in numbers on the two sides being wildly different and confusing. Sometime in the late 19th century the High Street was renumbered, starting at the east end, with odd numbers on the north side and even numbers on the south side. Hardly any of these numbers are shown on the buildings. Matching buildings to numbers is a difficult and imprecise science. Names of closes have changed over the years and many have no name plates. My apologies for any mistakes I have made.

Mary Byatt

Pont's Map of Elgin, c1593-1600.
Reproduced by permission of the Trustees of the National Library of Scotland.

Chapter 1: Origins

Elgin was founded alongside the small, steep, green hill at the west end of the present town on which the ruins of its castle stand. This hill was a natural fortress, protected on three sides by the winding course of the River Lossie and on the fourth side by a bog. The first record of a castle on the hill was around 1040, but the discovery of a carved Pictish cross-slab buried in the centre of Elgin suggests a much earlier settlement of the site. The first castle would have been constructed of earthworks and timber, and the first settlement would have been a cluster of wood and turf huts around the base of the mound.

David I of Scotland gained control over Moray in 1135 and he rebuilt the castle in stone.   Around this primitive 12th-century fortification, a trading centre and a hub of religious activity developed. Early Elgin was a typical medieval Scottish burgh, with just one street of houses, still made of either wood or turfs. This street was the Hei Gait, or High Street, and it extended from the castle to the east. The street widened in the centre to accommodate a market place where the tolbooth and burgh kirk were sited. Records of the kirk exist from the reign of William the Lion (1165-1214). It was probably thatched with heather, as were most country churches of the time. A mercat or market cross in the graveyard served as a gathering point for people and their wares. At that time it was usual to have markets in graveyards and remained so until the time of the Reformation. The first market cross has long since disappeared. The Muckle Cross now in the centre of Elgin is a much later structure.

Above: Two sides of the cross-slab known as the Elgin Pillar, now in the Cathedral

Above right: Ladyhill, Elgin

1

Burgesses of Elgin were allotted tofts or tenements of land that extended to the north and south of the High Street. These burgage plots were some 10 paces wide and 150 paces long. Known as 'lang riggs', there were up to 100 of them in the 13th century, supporting a population of 500-600. The medieval rigg pattern can still be seen, both on town plans and on the ground.

In 1224 the Bishop of Moray's seat was transferred to Elgin from Spynie and a magnificent cathedral was built to the east of the town, together with manses for the clergy. All were enclosed within the Chanonry wall. The town and the Chanonry were quite separate to begin with, but by the fifteenth century they were all but joined.

At the time when the Cathedral was built, the burgh had a thriving community of merchants and artisans and was one of the most important burghs in Scotland. In 1296 it was one of only four Scottish burghs given the title of 'city', the others being Aberdeen, St Andrews and Brechin. The population rose to 800 by the 14th century and in the 15th century it more than doubled.

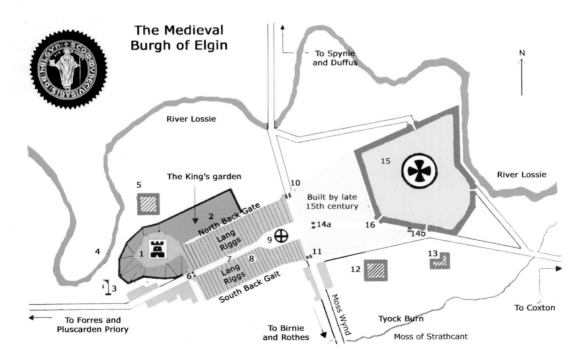

1. The Castle, now Ladyhill
2. The King's Garden
3. Gallows Green
4. Hangman's Ford
5. Blackfriars' Friary
6. West Port
7. The High Street
8. Thunderton House
9. Tolbooth, St Giles, & Mercat Cross
10. North Port in Carsemens Wynd
11. South Port, end of South Wynd
12. Greyfriars' Friary
13. Maisondieu
14. East Port, two positions, a & b
15. The Cathedral and Chanonry

Plan of the Medieval Burgh of Elgin, after Fenton Wyness (1944)

By 1400 Elgin had become a self-governing Royal Burgh with a population in excess of 1600. Burgess houses were now built of stone and mostly placed gable to gable along the High Street. They had three storeys, the third being in the roof, lit by dormer windows. Access to the 'backland' of the original toft was through a *pend* or arched passageway, protected by

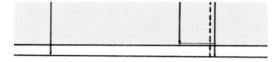

High Street

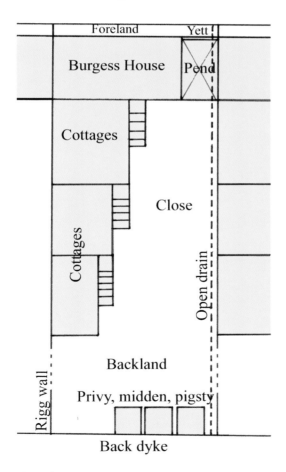

Plan of a medieval close, south side of High Street

a *yett* or gate. The backland provided stabling and space for a garden and small croft. It ended in a back dyke beyond which was common agricultural land, hence the present day Borough Briggs ('town riggs') to the north. The walls at the foot of the burgage plots formed the boundary of the Burgh of Elgin, and the Council decreed that they should be kept in good order.

As the population grew and more housing was needed, parallel rows of thatched cottages were built on the backlands, at right angles to the High Street. This created narrow alleyways off the High Street in a fishbone pattern. They became known as closes. There were often 10 houses per close, all built on the west side of each close, with doors and windows facing east, looking over the back walls of the next close. Thatching with heather was usual until 1735 when the practice was banned because of fire risk.

The size of the houses in a close diminished the further away they were from the High Street. An open drain ran along the east side, carrying waste water to the High Street. As late as 1954 most of the closes were still paved with cobbles.

Elgin is known to have employed surveyors ('linaris of land') around 1540 to supervise the laying out of streets and burgage plots. The town had four gates or ports that served more as customs points than for defence. The High Street ran from the West Port

Slezer's 'The Prospect of the Town of Elgine', 1693

beside Ladyhill along to the East Port which was now near the Bede house, beside the Chanonry wall. Running north and south from the High Street were two wynds containing the North and South Ports. The North Port was in Carsemens Wynd (see p.2). The South Port stood at the end of South Wynd, from where Moss Wynd led down to the undrained Moss of Strathcant. The Burgh Records of 1585 and 1600 describe how this small city prevented entry of strangers in order to protect itself from the plague. The roads and ports were simply blocked up with turfs - *'bigging ye wynds with faills'* (turfs) and *'bigging* (building) *and up-pitting the east and west ports'.*

The Elgin of the 15th to 17th century was still confined to one hundred yards on either side of the present High Street, and had a maximum of 175-200 closes. Slezer's *Prospect of the Town of Elgine in 1693* (above) shows buildings clustered along a ridge above the flood plain of the River Lossie. The town was described by Isaac Forsyth in *A Survey of the Province of Moray* (1798) as follows:

'The town consists of one principal street, in a winding course, for little more than a mile from east to west, widened to such breadth towards the middle of the town as to have the church awkwardly placed upon it, and at a distance farther on, the town-house, a mean building, adjoined to a clumsy square tower, almost without windows, which contains the hall where the courts and county meetings are held, and the common gaol.'

'Behind the houses which front the street, buildings are carried back on either side, in

The Tolbooth, containing the gaol, in 1820

narrow lanes, for the length of eight or ten dwellings, in some cases separate properties, and containing for the most part distinct families. Many of these lanes terminate in the gardens, affording more immediate access to the country than the few public avenues offer'.

The closes were often named after *'the distinct families'* living in them but sometimes were named after a trade carried out in them. Hence Founders' Close and Glovers' Close. Names changed with time. When the High Street was numbered, many of the old names fell out of use and some were lost altogether.

The names of the Wynds changed with time too. Carsemens Wynd, which led to

the North Port, became Shambles Wynd, site of the shambles or slaughterhouse. Later it became Lossie Wynd, as it was the main road north to Lossiemouth. At the beginning of the 20th century there was an attempt to change its name to Union Street. This name didn't stick and it reverted to being Lossie Wynd. A plaque marking the site of the North Port until 1787 can be seen today half way down Lossie Wynd on the east side. South Wynd, which led to the South Port, became School Wynd when two schools were built in it. From the mid nineteenth century it became the main thoroughfare to and from the railway station and its name was changed to Commerce Street. It contained two prestigious buildings, the Post Office and the Elgin Club. The South Port was removed as late as 1892.

As the wealth and importance of the ecclesiastical establishment grew, Elgin became an attractive place for Moray landowners to own property. They built town houses alongside those of the merchants. Some of the new town houses were on the land to the east of Carsemens Wynd, between the old city and the cathedral. Local lairds moved into their town houses for the winter with their families. One such town house was Elchies House (1670), owned by the Grants of Elchies. Like many others of that period it had an open arcade on the ground floor. It was originally built by the Cumines of Lochtervandich and Auchry, and was known first as Auchry's House. Ownership passed to King of Newmill and then to Grant of Elchies. Finally it was used as a boarding school by a Mrs Shand and then demolished in 1845 to make way for the building of a bank for the Caledonian Banking Company. The bank building still stands on the site today.

The 17th century was the great age of Scottish burgh architecture. The houses built in Elgin in that century had high roofs covered with grey stone slabs, often pierced by ornamented dormers bearing initials of the owner. Some houses had external stairs that gave access to rooms on the first floor. Many had *piazzas*, consisting of a series of arches supported by sturdy pillars, behind which ran a paved, covered walkway. The ground floor rooms were set back from the road and afforded little light to any trade carried on there. Braco's Banking House at No. 7 High Street is a surviving example of a *piazzaed* house. It was built in 1694 as a dwelling house and was bought in 1703 by William Duff of Dipple and Braco who turned it into a banking house. Two other examples of this style still exist; the buildings at Nos. 42-46 and at Nos. 50-52 High Street. Most of the 17th-century town houses were demolished in the first half of the 19th century to make way for large Victorian commercial buildings. The wealthy moved out to fine stone houses in the suburbs.

Elchies House

Leslie's House

Braco's Banking House

Elgin's 17th-century street architecture, R W Billings

Chapter 2:   Changing Times

Elgin's medieval town pattern lasted well into the 19th century, as Wood's map of 1822 shows. Shortly after this date a major transformation took place. The tight scale was broken by the construction of new streets leading off the High Street to the north and south. Calder House had just been demolished to make way for North Street. Now, on the opposite side of the High Street, John Batchen, owner of Thunderton House, feued   part of the policies to shopkeepers and tradesmen and Batchen Street was formed. At the same time Lossie Wynd was widened.

The High Street was to see further great changes in the 19th century. The parish church, described in 1798 as '*a low clumsy misshapen building, at once deforming and incumbering the street,*' was demolished in 1826.   It was replaced with a neo-classical building in the form of a Greek Doric temple.

Wood's 1822 Map of Elgin, marked with positions of old Town Houses

1. West Park, late 17th century
2. General Anderson's House
3. Elchies House, 1670
4. Thunderton House, 15th century
5. Calder House, 1634
6. Drummuir House, 1651
7. Ritchie's House, 1619
8. Vicar's Manse Ground and Garden
9. House of Leslie of Rothes, 1634
10. Unnamed *piazzaed* house, 1680
11. The Plough Hotel
12. House of Grant of Logie, 1776
13. St Duthac's Manse
14. Old Episcopal Church, 18th century
15. Donaldson's House, 1669
16. House of Innes of Coxton, 1677
17. Our Lady's High House, pre-reformation
18. House of Cumming of Lochtervandich, 1576
19. The Old Lodge, 1800
20. House of Anderson of Linkwood, late 1600s

Old St Giles Church, the Muckle Kirk

The Tolbooth

The *'townhouse'* or tolbooth, with its *'clumsy square tower'*, was taken down in 1843 and replaced by a fountain. The courthouse and county building were moved to the east end of the High Street and built on the site of the town house of Anderson of Linkwood.

The mid 19th century saw the demolition of much of Elgin's distinctive early architecture. The historian, Sheriff Cosmo Innes, described it as 'a veritable orgy of destruction', but Robert Young (*Annals of Elgin* 1879), wrote 'no town in the north of Scotland had made so much progress in the last 50 years'. A true historian, he devoted a whole chapter to describing the buildings that had recently disappeared. Illustrations of some of these lost houses can be found in scattered publications. They are collected together in the next pages and the map on the opposite page shows their position on the High Street. The official numbering of the High Street did not take place until the end of the 19th century and is given as a guide only to location of each house.

1. West Park, (late 17th or early 18th century), was a house built opposite Ladyhill by Robert Innes, grandfather of Sheriff Cosmo Innes. It had a large garden in which were grown *'all manner of fruits, among which were apricots of the best quality'*. Late in the 18th century, West Park was bought by Mr Francis Russell of Westfield. One night in 1783 he secretly pulled down the old West Port because it was in the way of improvements he wanted to make to his property. A violent dispute arose with the town authorities. Russell was fined £20, and the two masons responsible for the demolition were fined £3 and £2 and jailed for a week. Russell was given six months to rebuild the port, but somehow he avoided doing so and used the stone for his garden wall.

2. General Anderson's House, Nos. 205-7. General Anderson, who left money to build Anderson's Institution, lived in this house after he retired from India until his death in 1824. It was then bought by the Commercial Bank. The ornate façade, built in renaissance

The Commercial Bank, 205-7 High Street

palazzo style, was added in 1852. This flamboyant building was pulled down in 1960 to make way for the present, very plain, Royal Bank of Scotland building.

3. Elchies House (1670), Nos. 162-4, was a little west of Thunderton House, beyond the White Horse Inn. Young described it as *'a fine old building built on piazzas according to the ancient style, supposed to be borrowed from the Continent'*. It was demolished in 1845 and replaced by the

The White Horse Inn and Elchies House

Caledonian Bank, whose building is currently used by Ladbrokes, bookmakers.

4. Thunderton House was a large mansion built in the 15th century on 7 roods of burgh land, with grounds extending from the High Street right through to South Back Gait. It was used to accommodate royal visitors after the castle fell into ruins. Over the years it was added to and embellished but it did not escape the frenzy of demolition and change that took place in the 19th century. The property was purchased in 1800 by John Batchen, auctioneer, who took down large parts of the house, including the square tower shown in the engraving below.

5. Calder House (1634), Nos. 155-9, was built by Thomas Calder who was Provost of Elgin from 1665-1669. The doorway to the external stair tower bore the initials of Thomas Calder and his wife Magdalen Sutherland.

Thunderton House before 1800

Calder House

The inscription above the ornate tower door read:

'It is not cullors fair nor gold that gives the grace,
It is the verteous man adornes the dwelling place.
He that in youth no vertue useth
In adge all honours him refuseth.'

Ownership passed to relatives of the Sutherlands of Duffus and after that to a surgeon physician, Dr Alexander Dougal. The house was said to be haunted by his patients. One of them, Nelly Homeless, used to '*patter, patter up the long winding dark stair* [to the Doctor's study]*; give three knocks at the door, and all unbidden enter with grim unearthly look, and a huge*

gash in her breast, imploring back again her lights and liver, before she could find rest in her lonely grave'.

H B Mackintosh 1914

The poet, Will Hay (1794-1854), wrote:

'An' wailing ghosts were heard
In Dr Dougal's House, Sir;
Where deeds without a name
That made one's spirit grue, Sir!
Were done; but a' is gone
Since this auld coat were new, Sir!'

Calder House was demolished around 1820 to make way for a new street, North Street, and the Assembly Rooms.

11

The Assembly Rooms, The North of Scotland Bank (site of Drummuir House) and Ritchie's House

The Assembly Rooms, Nos 155-7, (above left) were built on the east side of North Street by the Trinity Lodge of Freemasons. They included a celebrated ballroom used by local gentry. The building was much mourned when demolished in the 1960s.

6. Drummuir House (1651), Nos. 151-3, was a classic late 17th-century three-storey house made of dressed ashlar, with *piazzas*. It was probably built by William King, Provost of Elgin. In 1723 it was sold to a Campbell of Cawdor who gave it to his daughter, the wife of Robert Duff of Drummuir. Thereafter it became the town house of the Duffs of Drummuir until it was sold in 1803 to the Incorporated Trades of

Elgin. They filled in the *piazzas*, made shops on the ground floor and a meeting room for the Trades on the first floor. This room was also used as a theatre, the 'Theatre Royal'. Sadly, no illustration of Drummuir House exists today. The North of Scotland Banking Company bought it in 1848 and demolished it to make way for the bank building in the centre of the old photograph above. It, too, has now gone. The much older house on the right was Ritchie's House, built in the style of 17th-century Elgin burgh houses.

7. Ritchie's House (1619), Nos. 147-9, was named after John Ritchie who owned it in the early 19th century. It is not known who originally built the house but in 1651 it was

Ritchie's House

into the ownership of Mr John Ritchie at the end of the 18th century. It was later used by Bailie Batchen as a shoemaker's shop, and finally it was left to the Magistrates of Elgin to be sold to endow the Ritchie Fund for poor people. When the house was demolished, its squat columns decorated with carved masks were used to make a loggia attached to Ladyhill House.

8. Vicar's Manse Ground and Garden, No. 115, was owned by the minister of St Giles in Roman Catholic times, but no evidence for an actual manse building exists. The property was split in the 19th century between John Forsyth, ironmonger, and Peter Nicholson, merchant. Nicholson sold his half of the property to the British Linen Company who built a bank on it. There was said to be *'a highly cultivated garden'* behind it.

owned by Bailie Robert Donaldson, who put his initials and those of his wife, Helen Culbock, over the windows. The initials of his son, John Donaldson, and wife, Catherine Urquhart, are over a huge stone fireplace that is preserved in a room on the first floor of the current building. The house passed through many hands before coming

9. Town House of Leslie of Rothes (1634). The remains of this house at No. 103 High Street is known as 'The Tower' because only the external stair tower is left from the original town house. It was said to have carried an ancient iron cross denoting ownership of the land by the Knights of St John, but this fact has never been substantiated. The house was later owned by Mr Isaac Forsyth, who had a large bookselling business and ran the north of Scotland's first circulating library from it, as early as 1789. After his death in 1839, the house passed to a Dr Mackay who rebuilt the

Carving above lintel of fireplace in Ritchie's House

The Tower, 103 High Street

main part in 1876, adding extra turrets. Later it was a shoe shop and then it became a temperance hotel.

10. An unnamed house, with *piazzas* (1680), No. 101. The original owner of this house is unknown; title deeds go back only as far as 1706. It had the initials 'IM' over the windows and passed through many hands before being demolished in the mid-19th century by Mr John Anderson. He replaced it with a house and shop. Another, large, early 17th-century house lay just beyond it to the east. Ownership of this second house passed through a succession

of merchants and the building existed at least until 1879.

11. Grant's House (1776), No. 114, stood opposite St Giles Church. It was built by James Grant of Logie, and was said by Young in the *Annals of Elgin* (1879) to be: *'... the largest house ever built in the burgh. ... There were two excellent shops fronting the High Street and a handsome gateway which conducted into a paved court within which was a large garden. ...The large building within the court was converted into two dwelling houses.'*

Towards the end of the 19th century it was sold to the City of Glasgow Bank and the front was covered with dressed ashlar. Two large ornamental windows and a big wing at the back were added. Today all that is left is a carved stone panel, dated 1776, set in the east wall of Harrow Inn Close, bearing the motto, initials and arms of James Grant.

Unnamed House with piazzas, 101 High Street

12. The Plough Hotel, Nos. 102-110, was an inn of long lineage, with stables at the back on South Back Gait. It was replaced in the late 19th century by the short-lived Palace Hotel. This Victorian building still exists. It is now known as the Palace Buildings and has two small shops on its ground floor.

13. St Duthac's manse, Nos. 96-8. St Duthac, the patron saint of Tain, was Bishop of Ross in the reign of Alexander II. After his death in 1249, St Duthac's Chapel in Tain became an object of pilgrimage. In pre-reformation times, St Duthac's Manse in Elgin may have been associated with a chaplainry within the parish of Elgin or used as a resting place for pilgrims on their way to Tain. The site was occupied later by the Fife Arms Hotel, and later still (in the late 19th century) by a hat manufacturer.

14. The Old Episcopal Chapel, No. 74, lay a little west of Commerce Street. It was built in the 18th century by a section of the church that acknowledged the House of Hanover. After 1788, when Charles Edward Stuart was dead, and political divisions were removed, the two episcopalian congregations amalgamated. The chapel was replaced in 1825 by a new church, built at the end of North Street. The old chapel became shops and warehouses. One of the shops was a haberdashers, tenanted by Mr Asher until the 1970s.

The Plough Hotel, 102-110 High Street

15. Donaldson's House (1669), Nos. 73-5, was a fine house with a *bartizan* (battlemented parapet) on the east corner of Lossie Wynd. It bore carved stones with the initials 'JD and JM 1669', for James Donaldson and Jean Mackean. The title deeds for the property go back to 1591, and the previous house on the site was said to have had an iron cross and may have been the preceptory of the Knights Templar. Donaldson's House was replaced as late as 1916 by the present day Union Buildings.

16. Town House of Innes of Coxton (1677), No. 53. The house bore the Innes star and had windows initialled 'AD' and 'ED', referring to later Duff ownership. William Duff of Dipple, father of the first Earl of Fife, lived here until 1722. Mr Robert Hay, cabinetmaker, built a large house on the site in the mid 19th century.

17. Our Lady's High House, No. 37, was an ancient house used by chaplains during the 16th century. One of them, Sir Thomas Ragg, ran a classical school in it and was ordered by the Town Council in 1546 to close it. The boys were made to attend the established grammar school. A very tall house can be seen in the correct position in Slezer's *Prospect of the Town of Elgine in 1693*, and this may have been Our Lady's High House. After the demise of Maisondieu hospital, it is thought to have been used by the sisters for feeding the poor. The property was bought in 1840 by the publisher Alexander Russell. He built the offices and printing works of The Elgin Courant here in the mid 19th century.

Cumine's House and The Old Lodge

18. Town house of the Cummings of Lochtervandich (1576), No. 13. Ownership of this property passed from the Cummings (or Cumines) to Innes of Leuchars. The last Innes to live there was a widowed old lady who would often be seen through the east arch, sitting beside the fireplace spinning lint. The building was demolished in 1893, along with the Old Lodge next door, to make way for St Giles, the large, grand building used now by the Morayshire District Ex-servicemen's Club. All that remains of the Cummings' town house is a carved stone shield bearing the inscription 'IC IC 1576', built into the wall high up near the front door.

19. The Old Lodge (1800), Nos. 9-11, was the first property of the Trinity Lodge of Freemasons. The ground was granted to them

in 1779 by their Grandmaster, Captain James Innes of Leuchars.   Later this house was lived in by Lachlan MacIntosh, who wrote the first *Elgin Past and Present*, published in 1891. His son, H B MacIntosh, wrote the more widely researched *Elgin Past and Present*, published in 1914. The house was bought by Dr Adam and later still by Dr Thow. The Old Lodge had a fine garden and the old stone arch in the North Port housing estate was within it.

20. The Town House of Anderson of Linkwood lay opposite Our Lady High House. There is no picture of it but it was said to be *'a good house of the old style'*. In 1834 it was sold to the Magistrates to make way for the new Courthouse. Its handsome gateway was taken down and re-erected at Pitgaveny.

Littlejohn's Close, No. 41 High Street

Chapter 3:   Elgin's Old Closes

Craigellachie Close (George Souter)

Elgin of the late 19th century was described by Charles Archibald in the Elgin Courant of 25.12.38 as *'a town of closes, with the greater part of its population living in houses tucked away up the narrow alleys which ran off the main streets'*. Archibald was brought up in a west end close. He was the son of a market gardener and became a school teacher. He wrote fondly of his memories. *'Every time I visit Elgin I enter its old closes and recall to mind some of the scenes and events of my early childhood – memories, many fond and dear, some sad and bitter, but even*

these last I would not be without for they, too, have helped to make me what I am. Without a doubt it was the humanising education of the close which created that "esprit de corps" common to us old Elgin "loons" '. [The inhabitants of a close] *'knew each other's ways quite intimately, each other's means or lack of means, each other's poverty, for all were poor'.*

Each close had *'a social life, a tradition, even an atmosphere of its own.'* Some closes *'took pride in their respectability, were scrupulously clean and tidy, with flowers and shrubs planted against whitewashed walls'.* Inside each house was a 'best room', kept for special occasions until overcrowding dictated that the space was needed for a growing family. Craigellachie Close was one such close. It was a clan close, belonging to the Grants and it got its name from a rough piece of Craigellachie rock on a pediment at the head of the close. Large numbers of families lived in Craigellachie Close: 32 in the 1851 census, 21 in 1881 and 15 in 1901. Several professions were practised in it. There were two shoemakers, two carpenters, a painter, a tailor and a vintner. At the head of the

Punchie Grant

close there was the shop of a barber and wigmaker. The last son of the owner of this

Ladyhill Close, with Ladyhill House in the background

business became one of Elgin's 'Worthies'. He was James 'Punchie' Grant, a shoemaker, born in 1794, the youngest of a family of 24. A much-loved man, he was best known for his prowess at fishing and the free meals he gave to the poor.

Other closes were not so clean. They *'flaunted their filth and their rags, their drunkenness, their immorality, their idleness.'* Archibald cites Gordon's Close as *'an unsavoury and slummy close where people, some of notoriously bad character, and some of queer traits or personal peculiarities lived'*. The closes around the foot of Ladyhill became particularly run down and were virtually the slum district of Elgin in Victorian times. Lady Lane had 28 families in 1881, living in 14 houses. It was here that the author and broadcaster, Jessie

Kesson (1916-1994), was brought up. Her novel *The White Bird Passes* (1958) describes life in Lady Lane in the 1920s. In one of her broadcasts, Jessie said: *'Life was:*
Eating when there was food;
Fighting when there was drink, and
All along a dirtiness,
All along a mess,
All along a finding out rather-more-
                                        than-less.'
Jessie was unsure whether she loved or hated the lane. She said she loved *'the friendliness of the kids; the fun of it all; the lamp-posts you climbed up playing at "Reliever!"*
.... Then there was the chip shop, with the smell that made one hungry; its constant hum of voices; its brightness and laughter, and the gramophone in the corner playing "Let the Great, Big World Keep Turning"'.

Scots Magazine, April 1942

In her book *Another Time, Another Place* (1983) Jessie Kesson wrote*:*

'One couldn't see much of the sky at the top of the close; and washing, endless washing, that never looked clean somehow, hung from one side of it to the other'.

Although life in a close as described by Jessie Kesson was never dull, it could hardly be described as comfortable. Every close had a communal tap, usually mid way along it. Jessie says she was *'forever running to the pump at the top of the close for water'.* Charles' Close at No. 95 High Street still has fittings of its communal tap half way down the close on the right hand side.

If the backland was used for growing vegetables, a close would be of just sufficient width for a farmer's cart to pass along. There was a common bleach green, a privy and a midden at the bottom end, and usually a pig-sty too. An open drain ran along the east wall and out into the open gutters that ran along each side of the High Street. Two common gutters crossed the High Street and carried filthy water down to the river Lossie. The largest of the common gutters was said to be beside the present day Royal Bank of Scotland,   and the second, smaller

Laing's Close (George Souter)

Dyster's Close (George Souter)

one, was near Lossie Wynd. The ancient High Street had a row of huge stone blocks along its centre, put there by Cromwell's men. On wet days people used these blocks as stepping-stones to keep out of the filth. The High Street was re-paved in 1822 and the drains covered over, but the gutters leading out of the closes were not covered until after a cholera outbreak in the 1850s.

George Souter (1845-1920), engineer and artist, painted a number of closes, showing their poverty. Most of the closes he painted have disappeared without trace.

The development of the High Street frontage left many of the backlands under-used and derelict, in stark contrast to the spacious and opulent Victorian buildings on the High Street. The low rents of property in those closes that did remain inhabited attracted working class tenants. They were overcrowded, had bad sanitation and lacked fresh air and daylight. The local press of the early 20th century contains several references.

The Elgin Courant of 11.10.1912 reported that *'There is one blot on the landscape and that is the existence of the closes flanking the High Street on both sides, and her working class dwellings in general. ...Into many* [closes] *the sun never directly shines and in some lamps are to be found burning at mid-day. ...Most* [houses] *are old, very old, and small and pokey. You stoop to enter, climb tortuous stairs not built for two to pass ...and find yourselves in wee boxes o' places. ...Often you come to a tenement and say to yourself "surely there can't possibly be more than two tenants here". Inquiry discovers four. A room and a bed closet, with perhaps a coal cellar under a stair thrown in, comprises the accommodation for a married couple and a small family'.*

Duncan's Close, No. 281 High Street

Nothing changed for the better during WWI, but, by the 1920s, consciences were stirring again. The Northern Scot of 21.2.1920 stated *'It is nothing short of tragic that such people should be compelled to live in these cheerless, unhealthy quarters'.*

From then on tenants were gradually moved out to new housing schemes on the edges of the town. Some, however, were content to stay on in the closes. In the same issue of The Northern Scot one old man was quoted as saying *'We hae been in hooses like these a' oor life, an' they're guid enough for us. They're nae bad hooses – it's the fowk that's in some o' them'.*

After WWII many more closes were vacated, left empty and became neglected. But some still remained inhabited, and as recently as 1974, the Lord Provost of Elgin determined that *'the rat-infested slums in the closes should be bulldozed to the ground and the tenants moved out'.*

Soon attitudes changed and conservation of old buildings was encouraged by government legislation. Re-habilitation of properties in the closes started but was fraught with problems. Standards imposed by Public Health Acts and building regulations were hard to meet. Some closes such as Littlejohn's Close, 41 High Street, were just demolished. The photograph of Littlejohn's Close shows how run-down it had become before it was knocked down in the 1960s. Once it was home to 14 families.

Elgin loons at entrance to Littlejohn's Close

Littlejohn's Close, No. 41 High Street

The Council established a revolving fund for re-habilitation of properties in the closes. Charles' Close and Forsyth's Close were developed into a neat, gated residential area but the fund does not seem to exist any more. Another fund, known as the Elgin Fund, was established by E S Harrison of Johnston's Mill in 1963. It paid for the restoration of Red Lion Close and Shepherd's Close (pp. 24-5 and 34-5). Murdoch's Wynd housing development, a tasteful and imaginative scheme, was awarded the top Saltire Award in 1985.

By far the greatest damage to Elgin's medieval heritage was done by the construction of the inner relief road to the north of the High Street. A relief road was proposed as early as 1945 but not built until the 1970s. The chosen route cut through the closes on the northern side of the High Street, parallel to the old North Back Gait. As a result even Charles' Close and Forsyth's Close are far shorter than they would once have been. Jack's Close (below) ceased to exist altogether. In all more than 50 old buildings were demolished, some of them listed by Historic Scotland.

Post card of Jack's Close, No. 267 High Street

Red Lion Close, No. 44 High Street
This was home to 15 families in 1881, falling to 9 by 1901. After WWII it had
become dilapidated and in need of renovation.

Shepherds' Close, No. 50 High Street

This close housed 3 families in 1851, 6 in 1881 and one fewer by 1901. It was renovated in the 1960s, along with Red Lion Close.

Braco's Banking House and the pend to Braco's Close

Chapter 4: The High Street Today: East End

The next three chapters record what is left of the closes in 2006, and describe some of the buildings that replaced Elgin's 17th-century town houses. The narrative is in the form of a walking tour. Follow the red line on the street plans to find your location.

Elgin Museum to Lossie Wynd (Section 1 to 2)

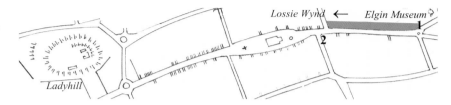

The Elgin Museum, 1 High Street   *D. Anderson*

To see the very best of Elgin's distinctive old architecture, start at the east end of the High Street, beside the Little Cross. Numbering of the houses starts here, with odd numbers on the north side and even numbers on the south side.

No. 1, **The Elgin Museum**, is an early Victorian Italianate building, specially designed by Thomas Mackenzie to house museum collections. It was opened in 1843.

No. 5, Braco's Close. Pass west of the museum to No. 3 High Street, currently a

coffee shop, and go through the *pend* into Braco's Close. Here is a living close, still housing several families. The four whitewashed cottages are 19th-century, developed from 18th-century dwellings. They retain the original crow-stepped gables. At the far end beyond the wooden trellis you will see another *pend*, but this is

Braco's Close, 5 High Street

probably of 19th-century origin. Once this close may have led to the 'Furlin' Yetts', a filthy narrow path that led east between two dykes and had turnstiles in it *'to prevent ingress of but one genus of animals'*.

No. 7, Braco's Banking House, lies to the west of Braco's Close and is one of Elgin's three remaining arcaded dwellings. It was

Dormer window of Braco's Banking House

built in 1694 as the town house of Innes of Coxton. It is a three-storey building, with traditional crow-stepped gables and a stone-slabbed roof. The stone slabs are known to have come from Leggat's quarry, Spynie. Look up at the dormers, which are pedimented and bear the initials 'ID' and 'MI' for John Duncan and Margaret Innes who built the house. Note the Innes star above Margaret's initials and then look at the skewputts (at the lower end of the crow-steps) where the initials are repeated. The house was bought in 1703 by the enterprising William Duff of Dipple and Braco, ancestor of the Earls of Fife. He carried on his banking business here until 1722. His town house was further west at No. 53 High Street. Originally the ground floor rooms would have been set back under the arches, forming a covered walkway that is sometimes referred to as a *piazza*. In the 1970s the banking house was renovated, both inside and out. The arcades, once bricked up, were restored and filled with plate glass windows. The first floor was found to have been a large baronial-type hall with a wall-to-wall fireplace at one end.

Nos. 9-11, St Giles. The building next to the west is the late Victorian building known as St Giles. It was designed by Andrew G Heiton in 1893 and is now used by the Morayshire District Ex-servicemen's Club. It occupies the site of two older houses, the Old Lodge (1800) and the town house of the Cummings of Lochtervandich (1576), later the property of Innes of Leuchars. High up in the wall near the front door is a carved stone shield bearing the inscription 'IC IC 1576'; all that remains of Cumming's old house.

The Cumming Arms on St Giles building, after H B Mackintosh, 1914

St Giles, 9-11 High Street

when it was fashionable to have open, arcaded ground floors. With binoculars you can see the date 1728 on the left hand skewputt of the first building and a carved face on the right hand skewputt. Also of interest is the unusual Venetian window, dated around 1750, on the second building in the group. The last two buildings were altered in 1852 by the addition of dormers.

The restoration of the Masonic Lodge buildings in 1971 was one of the first projects of the Elgin Fund. It won a Heritage Year Award of the Civic Trust in 1975. The complex of closes that used to exist behind the buildings is much altered.

Nos. 15-25, Masonic Lodge buildings.
Moving further west on the north side of the High Street you come to the only examples of eighteenth century burgh architecture in Elgin. In keeping with earlier Elgin buildings, these houses have crow-stepped gables but they were built after the age

No. 17, Masonic Close, is the first of two *pends* passing through the Masonic Buildings. Part of the old close wall exists next to St Giles. The *pend* leads to an area that has been much changed this century and is not recognisable as a close. Look for three heraldic carvings set into the walls. They

Venetian window

Mason Lodge Buildings

Masonic Close, 17 High Street

were rescued from a garden in North Street where they had lain for some years.   The one in the wall facing the *pend* bears the arms of Seton, Dunbar and Falconer and the initials 'A S'. Alexander Seton was Lord Provost of Elgin from 1591 to 1607 and became Lord High Chancellor for Scotland in 1604. He was created First Earl of Dunfermline and given the Bishop's Palace which he renamed Dunfermline House and extended.

Two more carved stones are set into the walls of the garden of Kilmolymock Close next door.

Family of Seton Arms, on wall in Masonic Close

Kilmolymock Close, 25 High Street

No. 25, Kilmolymock Close, is through the second *pend* to pass under the Masonic Lodge Buildings and, like Braco's, it is still inhabited. The houses are a storey taller than those in Braco's Close and are nicely renovated. Behind the hedge there is a length of the old 'dished' stone drain on the right hand side of the path, and two more carved stones, brought in from elsewhere and set into a garden wall. One of them, the one with two horses acting as bearers of the Elgin Fund's inscription, matches a carved stone in a low wall in Thunderton Place and is presumed to have been removed from Thunderton House when it was partly demolished by John Batchen. The complex of closes behind the Masonic Lodge Buildings once housed 25 families. Among these were a merchant, a tailor, a bottler and a carter.

No. 27-9, Founders' Close, gets its name from the foundry that operated here in the eighteenth and early nineteenth centuries.

Heraldic stone, inscribed 'The Elgin Fund 1971'

The bell-founder, Archibald Wilson, had workshops at the foot of the close. The close housed 11 families in 1851 and 12 in 1881. It is now closed off from the High Street and can only be entered through a private gate at the rear.

No. 37, Courant Court, lies between a solicitor's property shop (No. 35) and the Ionic Bar (No. 39). Once upon a time it was the site of an ancient religious house, Our Lady's High House (see p. 16). The site was bought in 1840 by Alexander Russell and he used it to build the office and printing press of Elgin's first newspaper, *The Elgin Courant*. The square *pend* is gated. Inside on the right are tall houses with bricked up doors and windows, followed by two

Inside Courant Court, 37 High Street

picturesque, inhabited cottages. The newspaper works were on the left.

Nos. 73-5, Union Buildings, on the corner of Lossie Wynd, bear a stumpy tower, dated 1916. This was presumably about the time when an attempt was made to rename Lossie Wynd as Union Street. The Union Buildings replaced Donaldson's House that was said by H B Mackintosh to be '*a fine specimen of the old architecture, lofty, and with a bartizan*'.

We now cross to the south side of the east end of the High Street.

The pend leading to Courant Court

Glover Street to
Commerce Street
(Section 3 to 4)

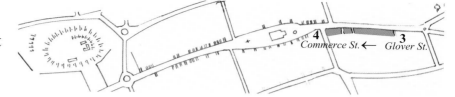

W alking west from the Little Cross on the south side of the High Street, the first suggestion of a close is a name only – **Glover Street.** It is all that is left of Nos. 8-10 Glovers' Close, which had two entrances. As well as being the site of Elgin's famous glove-making business, this close housed a coach-hirer and coachman in 1837. Census Records give 13 families living here in 1851, and then 8 families in 1881. William 'Birdie' Jenkins, one of Elgin's 'Worthies', lived in Glovers' Close from 1809 to 1885. He was a shoemaker who collected wild birds and allegedly taught them to sing popular songs.

Birdie Jenkins

Inside Forteath's Close, 30 High Street

No. 30, Forteath's Close. The *pend* to this close lies to the west of the Court House and

Next to Glover Street are the Courthouse and Council Buildings. The Sheriff Court (1864) was designed by Elgin architects, A & W Reid, and was described by contemporaries as *'more elegant than might be looked for in a city the size of Elgin'*. The first Town Council building was built a little earlier, in 1838, on the site of the town house of the Anderson of Linkwood. It was an elegant neo-classical building designed by William Robertson, A & W Reid's uncle. It was replaced after WWII by the current Moray Council building.

Dormer pediment on outer wall of Forteath's Close

Council Buildings and runs into a large car park. It was once an important pedestrian route through to the south and was home to 22 families in 1851, 20 in 1881 and 11 in 1901. Little remains of this once busy close, apart from the large square *pend*, and a pebble-dashed old rigg wall to the rear. In Victorian times the wall on the east of the *pend* was an open arcade. The arches have been filled in and decorated with four carved dormer pediments, from one of Elgin's 17th-century buildings.

No. 44, Red Lion Close, gets its name from the Red Lion Inn at its head, well known for

Nos. 42-46 High Street, the old Red Lion Inn

the visit of Dr Samuel Johnson and James Boswell in August 1773. The *pend* is vaulted and has been re-paved so the old drainage channel on the east side can no longer be seen. The close housed 15 families in 1881 and 9 in 1901. It was the site of the stables of the Red Lion Inn and later of Mr Jack's tallow candle factory. Another two of Elgin's 'Worthies' lived here. George 'The Garb' King rented a room

The Garb

Red Lion Close, 44 High Street

The pend of Red Lion Close

here from about 1810 until his death in 1845. He was an itinerant fiddler who paraded through the town in cast-off clothes of the gentry. The second was Peter 'Porridge' Laing who lived on a diet of oatmeal and died in 1890 at the age of 103.

The *pend* of Red Lion Close is through the central arch of the arcade of the Red Lion Inn, (see opposite). This large three-storeyed house dates from 1688. Its roof is covered in stone slabs.

No. 50, Shepherd's Close, lies to the west. The *pend* is through the first arch of a white, arcaded building, Nos. 50-52. Like the Red Lion Inn, it has its original dormers, crow-stepped gables and engraved skewputts.   The lip of the east skewputt is engraved '1694 AO' and the west '1694 JH AO' (Janet Hay and Andrew Ogilvie). Andrew Ogilvie was a merchant and Dean of Guild. The close has been re-paved and once had a lockable gate. The three-storeyed building inside on the left hand side may have been a warehouse. The cottages on the right hand side housed 3 families in 1851, 6 in 1881 and 5 in 1901.

The restoration of both these fine 17th-century houses, Nos. 42-46 and Nos. 50-52, won the Civic Trust Award in 1959. It was funded by the Elgin Fund. No more closes exist between here and Commerce Street to the west. Cross now to the north side of the city centre.

Shepherd's Close (above) and pend (below)

St Giles Church

Chapter 5: The High Street Today: City Centre

Lossie Wynd to North Street (Section 5 to 6)

British Linen Bank

In the first half of the 19th century, many of the old town houses, with their plain rubble walls, were replaced by dignified neo-classical buildings made of cut and polished stone. The 1830 British Linen Bank at No. 115 is an elegant example, with its parapet and square-headed windows. By 1850, the new wealth of the post-classical era gave rise to individual expression in the design of details on buildings, such as keystones and the paired Romanesque windows seen at No. 83 High Street. Major changes took place on both sides of the centre, but in spite of this it is still possible to make out the position of a number of the old closes. Some have been renovated and are lived in. All those on the north side have been shortened by development of the relief road. With the numbering of the High Street, some of the names of the closes have been discarded and forgotten.

No. 83 High Street

No. 87, Unnamed Close. The first close you come to on the north side, west of Lossie Wynd, has a very narrow gated *pend*, passing under a long, low building with roof level balustrade. Inside on the left is a row of four houses with two storeys,

No. 87 High St.

numbered 87A to 87D, and a little garden. At the end of the close there is an old wall surrounding a piece of waste ground that appears to be an old, un-used garden.

Unnamed Close, 87 High Street

Gordon Close, 91 High Street

No. 91, Gordon Close, has a narrow gated entrance that leads through a dark alleyway with bricked up windows and doors to a close of modernised, two-storeyed houses. A maximum of 14 families lived here in the 19th century.

Gordon Close, 91 High Street

No. 97, Charles' Close, is an early 19th-century close, which also has a very narrow entrance through a gated *pend*. Here again there are bricked up doorways and windows. Two of the first houses in the close have carved pediments over their doorways. Beyond are five modern houses. The close has name plates at both ends. The north end is gated too and is well short of what was North Back Gait. Look for an old stone drain made of dished stones which runs down the east side from midway to nearly the end of the close. Part way down there is a small stone pillar to which the old communal tap was fixed. Once there was a nail-maker's workshop in the close but it had closed by the time of the 1881 census.

Charles' Close, 97 High Street

No. 101, Forsyth's Close. Restoration of this close has been described as 'a textbook piece of work'. You enter it through a square, gated *pend*, a little west of Charles' Close. Windows of the houses on the east side are blocked up. Further down on the west side are several renovated and inhabited houses. In common with other closes, the size of the houses diminishes the further they are from the High Street end. You'll see that, first, there is a four-storeyed house, further down there are three two-storeyed houses, then two single-storeyed ones. The close interconnects with Charles' Close. It is gated and named at the lower end. Note the old drainage channel made of dished stones, running for a short way along the lower half of the east side.

The Tower, 103 High Street, and wall carving (inset)

In the mid 19th century Forsyth's Close was home to 6 families, including two tailors and a slater. It was also the site of St Giles Inn. Many years earlier, in 1713, Albert Gelly cast the big bell of the Tolbooth in Forsyth's Close. The bell is now in the Elgin Museum.

No. 103, The Tower. As already mentioned, this is just a small part of a house built by Alexander Leslie of Rothes in 1634. Look for the arms of Leslie and his wife on the wall of the Tower, beside the first floor window (see inset in photograph above). The rest of the building was 'baronialised' in 1876 by Dr James Mackay who lived here with his wife Margaret, his four children, a nurse, a cook and a maidservant.

Forsyth's Close, 101 High Street

The next section of the north side of the High Street has been extensively altered by the building of large banks and shops.   In the late 20th century you could still make out the backs of the old closes, but the construction of the shopping mall known as the St Giles Centre obliterated what was left of them. Fortunately the original 19th-century High Street frontage was retained.

Nos. 107-9, west of the Tower, is a post-classical building. It is described by Charles Mckean in his architectural guide as 'four storeys of bourgeois boasting, with a virtually transparent showroom on the first floor'. Next to it on the west side is an undated building with two dormers. It has been incorporated into the St Giles Centre and is a facade only.

No. 115 has six ornate urns crowning its parapet and the first floor boasts two dignified oriel windows.   It was built around 1830 as the British Linen Bank and occupies the site that was once the Vicar's

Urns on the British Linen Bank, 115 High Street

Ground Manse and Gardens. The bank building had 'a spacious vestibule' through which the entrance to St Giles Centre now passes. The W H Smith building to the west has three dormers decorated with thistles. Both these last two buildings are undated.

Nos. 123-133 to the west is a fine building called the St Giles Building, designed by R Baillie Pratt of Elgin. It was erected in 1904 for A L Ramsay & Sons, drapers.   Look up and you will see the initals W R (William Ramsay) and the date 1904.   Behind this building was Craigellachie Place.

Initials on St Giles Building, 123-33 High Street

Date on the St Giles Building

Nos. 137-9, the next building to the west, is a much older building from the first half of the 19th century. It has crow-stepped gables.

No. 137, Brander's Close, passes under the above building. Its gated *pend* is still there but it leads to a small area of blocked off waste land that is clearly not in use.

No. 141-5, dated 1876, is a very grand building, used until recently by solicitors, Stewart and McIsaac. There is an ornate pedimented doorway at the centre and a Greek key-pattern frieze to either side of it.

Nos. 147-9 was once the site of a house built in 1619. It was owned in the late 18th century by John Ritchie, whose descendants left it to the Magistrates of Elgin to endow a fund for the poor. When it was demolished in 1880, it was replaced by the current building with three ornate dormers, said to be 'in a similar style' to the 1619 house. There is a large, ancient fireplace from Ritchie's House on the first floor. The building is occupied by offices.

Nos. 147-9 High Street,
designed by A Marshall Mackenzie

Masonic symbol on 147-9 High Street

Elaborate, carved pediments on 147-9 High Street

The High Street in 19th Century

Clydesdale Buildings, 151-9 High Street

Nos. 151-9, Clydesdale Buildings

To the west, beyond the Victorian buildings, are the very plain 1970s Clydesdale buildings. The Clydesdale Bank replaced the 1857 North of Scotland Bank. This in turn had replaced the Trades Hall, which had once been the town house of the Duffs of Drummuir. The Clydesdale Store was built on the site of the Assembly Rooms, renowned for an elegant meeting room and magnificent dance floor. The photograph above left shows the Assembly Rooms and North of Scotland Bank. The building on the right of the bank is Ritchie's house, built in 1619 and demolished in 1880.

Elgin High Street in the second quarter of the 19th century

Commerce Street
to Batchen Street
(Section 7 to 8)

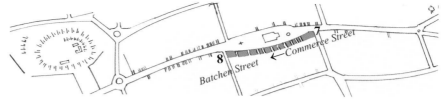

Moving on now to the south side of the city centre, you enter an area where there were once many hostelries: The Fife Arms Hotel (Nos. 96-8), the Plough Hotel (Nos. 102-108), the Star Inn (No.110-112), Harrow Inn (Nos. 112-4), the Gordon Arms Hotel (Nos. 118-122), the Newmarket Hotel (No. 130) and the Commercial Hotel (No.134). None of these now exists, although the Gordon Arms Hotel was open until 1980. On this south side you will see the only three full length closes that still remain. Starting from Commerce Street, on the South side, there are two Victorian buildings before you come to a close, the first is a three-story house with moulded windows and the second a two storeyed building with a roof-line balustrade.

Nos. 76-80 (c1830), the third building west of Commerce Street, has architraves and a cornice characteristic of the neo-classical period. It is a large four storeyed building and it spans Nicholson's Close. Doorways to either side indicate that there were once three closes here.

No. 78-80, Nicholson's Close, is the first close to the west of Commerce Street. Its square entrance, between two small shops, is part-closed by a plain, unpainted wooden door. Look for the fine wrought ironwork under the lintel above it. The *pend* is some 30 feet long and leads to a wide close with two houses on the right hand side, each with two storeys. They are divided into flats. Foundations for a new building have been dug beyond them. The ground beyond is derelict and there is no access to South Street. Five families lived here in 1881.

Nos. 82-86 was formerly the Union Bank. It has sculpted shell hoods above the first floor windows, ornate carvings above those on the second floor and is topped by a balustrade. It spans a living close.

Sculptured shells on Nos. 82-6 High Street

No. 82, Unnamed Close, belongs to Cockburns, solicitors. The vaulted *pend* leads to a courtyard of three storeyed houses, probably of mid 19th-century construction. There is a fine wrought iron gate with the initials CHY (for the solicitors Cockburn, Hamilton and Young) at the entrance to the *pend* and a carved head of a bull holding a lantern at the far end. Beyond is a mown lawn and behind that a small walled garden.

Unnamed Close, 82 High Street, Cockburns

Fife Arms Close, 92 High Street

No. 84, Hay's Close, is one of only three full-length closes passing from the High Street right through to South Street. The *pend* is through the left hand arch of the Bank of Scotland building. The 18th-century houses along it are all bricked up and it is used only as a pedestrian thoroughfare.

No. 92-100, Fife Arms Close, is the second pedestrian thoroughfare leading from the High Street through to South Street. It is named after the hotel that was once at its High Street end. There are two entrances to this close off the High Street. The first is through the right hand arch of the Bank of Scotland. Look out for an interesting

carved stone on the south gable of the house at the junction of the two parts. The 1901 census records 3 families living in the close at No. 92, and 6 in No. 100.

Pediment from old dormer, Fife Arms Close

No. 94 is a post-classical Victorian building with dormers and cast iron railings. It is less pretentious than most of its period.

Nos. 96-98 was the site of the Fife Arms Hotel and, before that, St Duthac's Manse. The hotel's stables were at the South Street

Nos. 112-114, Harrow Inn Close, passes under the end of the 1970s building and is the third pedestrian way from the High Street through to South Street. The *pend* shows evidence of having been gated. The first building in the close was The Harrow Inn, dated 1766. Behind it are 14 terraced houses with crow-stepped gables, mostly with two storeys. Several carved stones are to be found in the close, including the arms and initials of James Grant of Logie. They are all that is left of Grant's house, built in 1776 and said at that time to be the largest house ever to be built. There is also a carved moulding, a vaulting boss and a gargoyle set into the east wall. Above them is a marriage

The Palace Buildings, 106 High Street

end of Fife Arms Close and Elgin's first cinema, The Picture House, was built there in 1926.

No. 106, Palace Buildings. This was the Palace Hotel which replaced the Plough Hotel, a hostelry of long lineage. The Palace Hotel lasted a very short time and the building now houses small shops.

Nos. 110-114 is a plain 1970s building occupied by Boots (just showing on right of above picture). It was once the site of the Star Inn and the Star Inn Close and of the town house of James Grant of Logie.

Harrow Inn Close, 112-4 High Street

Carved stones, Harrow Inn Close

Dalmeny Place, 124-132 High Street

stone dated 1668 and inscribed with the motto 'NULL CERTUS DOMUS' *(no man's home is certain)*. On the opposite side of the close is another marriage stone, over a window that was once a door. It is carved 'AA MZ 1620' and 'AS MG 1725'. The next building to the south has moulded windows upstairs and a skewputt dated 1766. The close is used for small commercial businesses.

Nos. 118-122 was once the Gordon Arms Hotel. The ground floor has been converted into two large shops.

Nos. 124-132, Dalmeny Place (1848), is a grand building with semi-circular pediments above each of its seven first floor windows and wall-head chimneys linked by a balustrade. This building is clearly visible in the 1859 painting marking the celebration of Burns' centenary. On the right hand side of the first floor there was once a theatre and behind it the Cornmarket Hall that was used by the Rifle Volunteers as a drill hall and armoury.   It was supported on strong stone pillars that formed stalls for fleshers and greengrocers on the ground floor market.

No. 130, Newmarket Close, is an arched passage with a vaulted ceiling resting on eight pairs of strong pillars.   The arches between the pillars are now all bricked up but they once held the stalls of the 19th century New Market. The market was on two levels, and went right through to South Street, where there is a grand arched entrance. Charles Archibald (see Chapter 3) used to run through here in the 1870s, on his way

Roof Line, old Gordon Arms Hotel

Newmarket Close, 130 High Street

from the west end of the town to the Infant School in Frances Place. Sixty years on, he vividly described the market in his 1938 article for the magazine of the London Morayshire Club. He remembers in detail the stalls and their colourful owners, starting with a butcher's shop on the left and 'Fish Bawbie's' shop on the right.

Newmarket Close was developed in 1851, probably from an earlier close known as Stephen's Close. Coins of the realm and a record of the opening of the New Market are buried in its foundations. The close now leads to a public house and a nightclub and on the South Street end there is a shop. To the west is Batchen Street, built in the 19th century and not part of the medieval pattern. It was once part of the policies of Thunderton House (see pp. 47-50).

Elgin High Street on the occasion of Burns' Centenary in 1859.
Note the fountain which replaced the Tolbooth, and Dalmeny Place behind it.

Chapter 6: The High Street Today: West End

Batchen Street to
Northfield
Terrace
Section 9 to 10

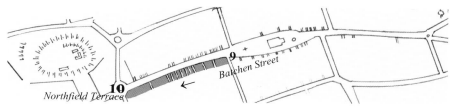

Thunderton House, 150 High Street

With a view of ending up at Ladyhill, we'll now walk the south side of the west end first instead of the north. Batchen Street is the eastern limit of the policies of Thunderton House, that once 'Great Lodging' or Kings' House where monarchs stayed from the late 14th century onwards when visiting Elgin. At one time its gardens, orchards and bowling green extended from the High Street to South

Back Gait and occupied the width of seven burgage plots. The original charter was granted to Thomas Randolph by his uncle, King Robert the Bruce. In 1455 the property passed by forfeiture to the Dunbars of Westfield. Some time after 1603 it was back in the hands of the Earls of Moray and then sold in 1650 to the Sutherlands of Duffus. Lord Duffus enlarged it and added a squat tower with a *bartizan* and balusters representing the letters 'Sutherland'. Prince Charles Edward Stuart was said to have stayed here with 'an inflammatory cold' for some days before the battle of Culloden in 1746. Some fifty years later the property was bought by Mr John Batchen, an auctioneer, whose wife had worked as a maid in the house in 1746. Batchen altered Thunderton House extensively. He turned it into a mill and a preaching house and feued the eastern part forming Batchen Street.

Carving on Thunderton House

'Mr Haldane's Church' was built on the High Street frontage. The squat tower and west wing were taken down in 1822 to make room for the construction of Batchen Lane. All that remains of Thunderton House belongs to the late 17th century. Its walls are liberally decorated with carved stones from previous buildings. The dormers at the back are original. It is now an inn and is hemmed in behind High Street shops. A carved stone in a low wall near the front of Thunderton Place matches a stone set into a wall in Kilmolymock Close. It depicts two rearing horses as supporters of a coat of arms, but the arms are missing. The two stone savages from either side of the front door are in the Elgin Museum.

Closes to the west of Thunderton House are not very obvious from the High Street, many of them having been blocked off. But if you climb up onto the upper terrace of the car park behind, you get a good view of the

The White Horse Inn, 160 High Street

closes on the south side of the High Street from behind. They are all very truncated, having had their southern-most ends cut off when Batchen Lane was built.

No. 160, White Horse Close, leads through to Batchen Lane. The White Horse Inn on the High Street has a modern, harled frontage, but the close to the rear is 17th-century. The sidewalls, stable and stone slabbed roof are original.

This close was home to Alexander Gray who left £20,000 when he died in 1807 for a hospital *'for the sick and the poor in the town and county of Elgin'*. His father was a

Carved heraldic stone from Thunderton Place

The White Horse Close, 160 High Street

William Hay wrote the following, published in the '*Lintie of Moray*':

'Her name is Mrs Innes and the 'White Horse' is her sign,
And happy is the man or beast that chances there to dine;
For all her provender is good, her whisky, ale and wine;
An' each an' a' hae often turned this weak, weak head o' mine;
O! she's a jewel o' a guidwife, the pride of Elgin Toon.'

Nos. 162-6 is a stately building beyond the White Horse Inn to the west. It was erected as the Caledonian Bank in about 1845, on the site of Elchies House, one of Elgin's 17th-century arcaded town houses. It is now the premises of Ladbrokes, the bookmakers.

wheelwright and a watchmaker by profession. Alexander followed his mother's side of the family into the medical profession and qualified as a doctor in Edinburgh. In 1780 he was appointed assistant surgeon in the service of the Honourable East India Company and made his fortune in Calcutta. The foundation stone of Dr Gray's Hospital was laid 1815, on the day that news of victory at the Battle of Waterloo arrived.

The White Horse Inn had a very popular hostess for 51 years in the 19th century.

White Horse Close from car park above TK Maxx

Seceders' Close, 166 High Street

Cooperie Fraser's Close and carved lintel of pend

No. 166, Seceders' Close, is not inhabited. It is blocked off by a blue wooden door on the High Street and can only be viewed from the upper floor of the car park behind. The cobbles are original and there is still a drain down the east side. It was an early close, with houses dating from the 17th century. All are now gone. 13 families lived here in 1851, 15 in 1881 and 18 in 1901. Dr Mora Scot, an Elgin GP of many years' service, remembers visiting families in this close in the early 1940s. She says there were at least 4 houses (A B C & D), each with

four families. A central doorway led to four dwellings. A stairway led to two upstairs dwellings and a passage to left and to right led to two downstairs dwellings. The passages ended in a single room with a bedroom area off it. A whole family lived in each of these small spaces. The only plumbing was to an iron sink. The privy was outside.

No. 176, Cooperie Fraser's Close, has mainly 18th-century cottages with 1½ storeys and dormer windows in the roof. At

The Pend of Kyle's Close, 184 High Street

the back of the *pend* there is a marriage stone above the lintel dated 1682 and carved with the initials 'IG WH' in a complex monogram (see inset in photograph, p.52). There were 20 families registered here in the 1851 census, 15 in 1881 and 16 in 1901.

No 184, Kyle's Close. A gated *pend* leads to an old cobbled courtyard with 5 two-storey 19th-century houses. The gate is locked at night. There were 14 families living here in 1881. At one time it was the property of Bishop Kyle of Aberdeen.

No. 190, Laing's Close. The whole close is inaccessible from the High Street and only

Inside Kyle's Close

Unnamed Close, 204 High Street

visible from behind. A mason and a builder had their workshops here in 1837. There were 9 families in the close at that time. Cant's *Old Elgin* records evidence of moulded doorways on some houses in 1945.

No. 204, Unnamed Close. This close is concealed behind the entrance to the restaurant, Qismat. Even from the back it is not very obvious. Three families lived here in 1851 but it is not mentioned in later censuses.

No. 206, Deacon Laing's Close. A once-gated close with a fine piece of wrought ironwork just below the lintel of the *pend*.

Clark's Close, 210 High Street

Inside is a narrow close with 19th-century two-storey houses. In 1881 7 families lived in it and in 1901 there were 10 families. The three-storey houses are numbered 206, then 206 A, B and C.

No. 210, Clark's Close. This close can be identified by a carved stone with the initials 'JM' and dated 1827 above the lintel of the *pend*. It is owned by Smillie's, the bakers who have a shop at No. 212. The stairs that can be seen through the *pend* lead to a first floor flat. The close is blocked off behind the stairs. The entrance shows signs of having been gated.

Deacon Laing's Close, 206 High Street

Lintel of 210 High Street

Clark's Close, 210 High Street

No. 214, Seivewright's Close. A narrow close with houses with blocked-off doors and windows. All are business premises and none is lived in nowadays. But 7 families lived here in 1851, 6 in 1881 and 5 in 1901. The houses are mainly two-storey, and the roof of the house above the *pend* may be 17th-century. There is a cemented drainage channel on the east side.

Seivewright's Close, 214 High Street

No. 224, Unnamed Close, has a fine wrought iron gate across the *pend* and an old stone drain along the east side. The *pend* leads to waste land at the back, with a stair on the right to the first floor flat above the *pend*. Just beyond is Northfield Terrace.

Un-named Close, 224 High Street

North Street to
Ladyhill
(Section 11 to 12)

Starting again at North Street, the first building you come to on the north side of the High Street was once a grand bank. **No.161-165, Woolworths,** is an Italianate building, built for the Royal Bank in 1856. It is a fine specimen of mid-19th century architecture. It has since been much altered on the ground floor and sadly the upper floors are in a very bad state of repair.

West of Woolworths are the remnants of many closes, some without nameplates.

No. 167, MacIllraith's Close, is a gated close without a nameplate, entered through

Woolworths, 161-5 High Street

Round stair towers, 167 High Street

an arch west of Woolworths. The buildings at the head of the close are early 19th-century, and have two upper storeys. They are served by round stair towers which can only be seen from behind a metal gate at the back of the *pend*. One stair leads up to a tailor's and the other to a hairdresser's. The close contains a couple of buildings, used for commercial purposes, and it is blocked off beyond them.

No. 175, Walker's Close, was home to 14 families in the mid 19th century. From 1884 to 2004 it was the premises of Elgin's newspaper, The Northern Scot, and the close was not accessible. Today there is a health food shop at the High Street end, a

City Arms Close, 185 High Street

proposed restaurant at the north end and the close between them has been opened up.

No. 181, Jack's Close. The *pend* to this close is beside the Ca'Dora fish restaurant. It is gated and locked. Once 13 families lived here, but now it is deserted.

No. 185-187, City Arms Close, is two separate closes that were re-developed in the 19th century and are now linked together. In No.185, the houses are 19th-century terraced houses and some have outside stairs. It is blocked by a pub at the north end. No. 187 goes right through to the relief road,

Jack's Close, 181 High Street

past the nightclub, Joannas, and the Playhouse Cinema. The remains of a stone arch can be seen on the east wall of the *pend*. The last houses in the close, Nos. 187 F & G, were demolished to make way for the relief road.

No. 203, Unnamed Close. There are seven, two-storey 19th-century houses in this close, numbered 203A to 203G. All are inhabited.

No. 205, Reid's Close, lies to the east of the Royal Bank of Scotland. You can't see into it because it has been blocked off by walls and gates connected to the bank. Some say that the common gutter taking dirty water

off the High Street down to Borough Briggs ran through here.

Nos. 207-9, Royal Bank of Scotland. This was once the site of the house of General Anderson, the benefactor of Anderson's Institute at the east end of Elgin (see p.10).

No. 211, Victoria Close, is a long close running right through to a car park beside the relief road. It is adjacent to the Victoria Bar and was probably re-named in the late 19th or early 20th century. There is a row of six two-storey terraced houses and three 1½ storey cottages; mostly 19th-century but with parts dating back to the 18th century. In 1954 there was a stone-slabbed roof with

Victoria Close, 211 High Street, looking north   *Victoria Close, looking south*

high set dormers, and, as recently as 1978, the close was still paved with cobbles. Look for the old *rigg* wall on the right hand side at the north end. It is perhaps the best surviving example of a boundary wall. Victoria Close was a busy close with 15 families living in it in 1881.

No. 227, Duffus Close, is built up at the High Street end and only accessible from the side of the Marks and Spencer car park. The houses are numbered towards the High Street instead of away from it, in the opposite direction to most closes. Numbers 2 and 3 occupy a fine four-storeyed building which has been renovated by the Elgin Fund.

No. 229, Innes Close. Blocked off by a locked door on the High Street and only accessible from the rear via Miller's Close.

No. 233, Miller's Close, is also still inhabited. It is a long, gated close with evidence of a drain along the east side. It was one of several closes which linked through to Murdoch's Wynd to the west. It had a row of two-storey, 17th-century houses, with lintels dated 1671 and 1681. There are six houses and the last two have dormer windows. Miller's Close was home to 9 families in 1851 and 1881 and one fewer in 1901.

No. 237, Unnamed Close. This is the last *pend* on the north side of the High Street before the ring road roundabout. The east wall only remains, being the backs of houses of the next close to the west. These houses are a fine example of the decrease in size of houses in a close, the further away they are from the High Street. The lintel over the back end of the *pend* bears a remarkable carved stone dated 1686. It has two trade symbols on it. On the left are the crown and hammer of the Hammermen and on the right

Miller's Close, 233 High Street

The north end of Miller's Close

termed the 'Victorian slum district' of Elgin. The development won the top Saltire Award in 1985.

A WWI Memorial Garden lies at the foot of the steps leading up to the monument on Ladyhill. It was donated in 1918 by Sir Archibald Williamson, MP for Moray and Nairn and comprises two war veterans' cottages, named Sulva and Messines, and a garden *'in commemoration of the termination of the Great War'*. Each cottage has a sheltered arcade incorporating old carved stones, perhaps collected by the architect Thomas Mackenzie from old town houses. He lived in Ladyhill House above.

No. 295, Hill Terrace (formerly Lady Lane), was the site of a coach-builder's business in 1837. It housed 19 families in 1851 and 28 in 1881. It was renamed Hill Terrace in the re-development of the 1980s. Some of the 19th-century buildings remain along the west side. The 20th-century author, Jessie Kesson, lived in Lady Lane (see p.19). High above on the green mound,

Unnamed Close, 237 High Street

Trade symbols above the lintel of No. 237

the goose (or iron) and scissors of the Tailors' Guild. The stone came from a former building on the site.

Ladyhill. Beyond the roundabout there is a tasteful development in place of the old closes at the foot of Ladyhill. This was the most run-down and dilapidated area of Elgin and formed what one writer has

Hill Terrace, formerly Lady Lane

which Jessie regarded as her personal playground, are the ruins of Elgin Castle, whose buildings were burnt in 1297. The stone keep and chapel dedicated to the Virgin Mary were maintained for at least another 150 years. The hill is now dominated by the memorial to the fifth and last Duke of Gordon, a revered benefactor of the area.

'The Duke of Fife's Hill [stet]*, willed as a playground for the inhabitants of the town, became peculiarly our possession. It loomed above the Wynd; the stone effigy of the aristocratic Duke gazing down on us with an indifferent eye.'*
Jessie Kesson, *The White Bird Passes*.

So what does the future hold? From the top of Ladyhill, you can see what is left of Elgin's medieval burgh pattern. It has survived the ravages of the mid 19th and mid 20th centuries. Let's hope that the mid 21st century will not bring another wave of destruction of old buildings. Few people live in the Georgian and Victorian buildings of the city centre and they are sorely in need of repair. The city centre has been drained of its life-support. Retail outlets built on the outskirts have slashed the number of small shops in the centre. But what is left of Elgin's closes could still be upgraded and promoted as a significant tourist attraction.

Elgin High Street, c1990　　　*P & A Macdonald/Aerographica.*

Index

Bibliography

Archibald C, 1938, *The Elgin that I lived in 60 years ago*, Journal of the London Morayshire Club.

Archibald C, *Life in the Closes*, Elgin Courant and Courier, 25.12 1938.

Bishop B, 2002, *The Lands and People of Moray, The Closes of Elgin*.

Bishop B, 2002, *The Lands and the People of Moray, Part 6, The Burgh of Elgin in the 17th Century*.

Bishop B, 2002, *The Lands and the People of Moray, Part 7, The Burgh of Elgin in the 18th Century*.

Bloomfield T C, 1978, *Conserving Elgin's Closes*, Department of Conservation, Heriot Watt University.

Cant, R G, 1946, *Old Elgin, A Description of Old Buildings*, The Elgin Society.

Cant, RG, 1954, *Old Elgin, A Description of Old Buildings*, The Elgin Society.

Cant, R G, 1974, *Historic Elgin and its Cathedral*, The Elgin Society.

Cramond, W, 1908, *The Records of Elgin 1234-1800*, Aberdeen.

Mackintosh H B, 1914, *Elgin Past and Present*, J D Yeadon, Elgin.

Mackintosh, Lachlan, 1891, *Elgin Past and Present: A Guide and History*, Black, Walker, Grassie, Elgin.

McKean, C, 1987, *The District of Moray, An Illustrated Architectural Guide,* Scottish Academic Press.

Murray, Isobel, 2000, *Jessie Kesson, Writing her Life*, Canongate Books Ltd.

Pride, Glen, 1975, *Glossary of Scottish Building*, Famedram Publishers Ltd.

Seton, M, 1980, *Elgin Past and Present*, Moray District Libraries.

Rhind, W, 1839, *Sketches of Moray*, Edinburgh.